Psychic Development

A Beginner's Guide to Developing Psychic Abilities

Lauren Lingard

Table of Contents

Introduction: The History of Psychic Development 1

Chapter One: The Different Psychic Abilities and How to Develop Them 4

Chapter Two: How to Have a Third Eye Awakening 8

Chapter Three: The Art of Psychic Mediumship 11

Chapter Four: The Energy of Reiki and Other Healing Modalities 13

Chapter Five: Psychic Readings from a Divinatory Lens 16

Chapter Six: The Psychic World from an Astrological Lens 19

Chapter Seven: Automatic Writing and its Modern Uses 25

Chapter Eight: Healing Crystals and Colored Stones 29

Chapter Nine: Divination Continued: Tarot Card Reading 32

Final Words 50

Introduction: The History of Psychic Development

The word "psychic" comes from the Greek word "*psychikos*" ("of the mind" or "mental") and speaks of the human mind or psyche. This particular Greek word can also mean "soul." In Greek mythology, the maiden Psyche both personified and deified the human soul. The Latin derivative of "psyche" is from the Greek word "psyche," which means "breath," and comes from "psychein," meaning to "breathe" or "to blow."

The French astronomer and spiritualist Camille Flammarion is known for first having used the word "psychic," whereas it was later brought about in the English language by Edward William Cox in the 1870s.

Initial systems of fortune-telling and divination were introduced in ancient times. The most well-known system of early fortune-telling was astrology, where those who practiced it believed that the positioning of celestial orbs could provide either future or present insight into their lives. Certain fortune-tellers were also able to make predictions without the usage of any of these systems. They claimed to be able to predict the future through visions or another kind of direct means. These types of individuals were known as seers or prophets, and later on, they were known as clairvoyants (which is the French word for "clear sight" or "clear seeing") and psychics.

Seers, however, also played a vital role in early civilization, given that they acted as advisors, priests, and judges. Various instances are included in the Bible. The Book of 1 Samuel (Chapter 9) depicts this when Samuel is requested to find donkeys of the future king Saul. The prophetic role appeared consistently throughout ancient cultures. In Egypt, for example, the priests of the sun deity Ra at Memphis behaved as seers. In ancient Assyria, seers were known as "*nabu*," meaning "to call" or "to announce."

The Delphic Oracle is one of the earliest and most classical stories of prophetic abilities. Pythia, the priestess who was presiding over the Temple of Apollo at Delphi, was thought to be able to come up with prophecies that were inspired by Apollo during rituals that started in the 8th century B.C. It is frequently thought that Pythia came up with oracles in a frenzied state of mind, induced by vapors that were rising from the ground, and that she spoke gibberish, thought to be the voice of Apollo, which priests remolded into the mysterious prophecies that were beheld in Greek literature. Many scholars think that records from the time suggest that Pythia spoke clearly and intelligibly, providing prophecies in her voice. Pythia was a position that was served by a succession of women who were more than likely chosen from a group of priestesses of the temple. The last response that has been recorded was provided in 393 AD, which is when the emperor Theodosius I ordered pagan temples to be destroyed. More recent geological investigations suggest that perhaps ethylene gas caused Pythia's state of inspiration.

One of the most significant historical findings regarding psychic abilities is the prophetic abilities of Michel de Nostredame. Nostredame was a French apothecary and seer who wrote collections of prophecies that have since been made famous on a worldwide level. He is most well-known for his book *Les Propheties*, which first appeared in 1555.

In the mid-nineteenth century, Modern Spiritualism became well known in the United States and the United Kingdom. The movement's most distinctive feature was the belief that the spirits of the dead were able to be contacted by mediums in order to provide insight into the world of the living. The movement was particularly propelled by anecdotes of psychic powers. Daniel Dunglas Home was especially thought to have psychic abilities, and he gained influence during the Victorian era for his ability to talk to the dead and levitate.

While the Spiritualist movement grew, so did other groups, such as the Theosophic Society, which was co-founded in 1875 by Helena Biavatsky. Theosophy, joined with spiritualist elements of Eastern mysticism, was influential in the early-20th century, and later impacted the New Age movement throughout the 1970s.

By the late 20th century, psychics were most commonly connected with New Age culture. Psychic readings and advertising for psychics became popularized from the 1960s and on, as readings were given for a fee and at home, over the phone, or at fairs.

Chapter One: The Different Psychic Abilities and How to Develop Them

As a practice, the phenomenon of psychic abilities has been commonly questioned by society, science, and culture as a whole. There are, however, instances during which any type of perceived psychic talent can be thought of as a true spiritual gift or calling from a supernatural force. Since science and spirituality are frequently at odds with one another, it can be difficult for science-minded, more rationalist thinkers to accept any sort of psychic ability, but there are undeniable occasions during which psychics have provided true, accurate, and factual information. Although the sources may be unknown to scientists (or to the psychics themselves), the psychic gifts are nevertheless real, and are known as the following:

- Clairvoyance: also known as "clear seeing," this particular ability involves the perception of visions in the third eye (mind's eye located in the middle of the forehead). Clairvoyant mediums see images that flash mentally in the form of people, scenes, places, objects, spirits, symbols, colors, and so on.

- Clairaudience: also known as "clear hearing," this is the gift of hearing messages from the divine spiritual realm. Messages come from this realm and are passed on directly to one's mind. At times, voices may call out specific names or messages that are similar to hearing mixed messages on a radio.

- Clairempathy: also known as being an "empath," or displaying extraordinarily strong levels of empathy. It also includes sensing or feeling emotions from other individuals or from spirits. Empathic mediums can easily detect the emotions of others such as happiness, joy, sadness, anger, and fear.

- Clairsentience: this is also known as having strong gut feelings or intuition, and it relates to being an empath in some respects. With this ability, one will be able to experience both positive and negative emotions from others. The feelings are typically being passed on from spirit guides and differ very strongly from one's own emotions.

- Clairalience: the gift of being able to detect scents or odors that are being passed on from the spiritual realm. Typically, the other individuals in the room are unable to smell these scents. It can, for instance, be a message from a spirit that is related to the particular smell (such as the scent of tobacco from a person who was a heavy smoker when alive).

- Clairgustance: the ability to "taste" the messages that are being passed on by spirit guides. Spirits are able to pass on behaviors or influences from past people in our lives and at times, it can come in the form of tastes or flavors. Typically, this will come in the form of something that this person appreciated while he or she was alive.

- Clairtangency: also known as psychometry, this means that a message will be transmitted to one if touching or holding an object in one's hands. One with this ability can usually detect information regarding the individuals who had once been living and had owned these particular objects.

Essentially, it is thought that everyone has some sort of psychic ability; it is all about whether one would like to refine or develop these abilities or gifts/senses. They are similar to the five senses that observe the physical world but relate to things occurring in the spiritual world. Some instances of psychic senses at work in the world around us are: being aware that someone will call us, thinking of someone and then shortly running into him or her, dreaming of events that go on to occur in reality, and meeting someone and then having a feeling about him or her that is later authenticated.

In order to develop our psychic abilities, we must first, as previously mentioned, come to the realization that we all are inherently blessed with some sort of psychic ability. It is important to keep in mind that we are not learning anything new, but are reopening these abilities from where they had been hidden inside of us. The psychic senses are linked to the intuitive, creative, and empathic parts of our brains (the right side), so if we would like to tap into these senses, then we need to silence the more analytical, logical, and mathematical aspects of our brains (the left side). If we spend time overthinking, or being overly logical, then we overpower our sense of "inner knowing," or sixth sense that we all inherently possess.

One of the most challenging, yet efficient, ways of making our psychic abilities stronger is through meditation. Meditation is a stress reliever, but it is also a way of improving sensitivity to the various 'clair' senses. Energy can be considered the "language of spirit," and spending time contemplating our thoughts, feelings, and dreams can enable us to get in touch with our psychic abilities. Whenever we spend time reflecting on life and our own spiritual selves in a deep and empowering way, we enable our intuitive, emotional sides to communicate as well as be listened to by the world around us.

In an external sense, being in nature raises our vibrations (the feeling of being lighter, happier, and more spiritually attuned), and in order to connect with the spiritual world, psychics are encouraged to remain in this state of high vibration. A walking meditation through the woods, for instance, will help our psychic senses to pay closer attention to the minute sounds of the energies of the trees, plants, and animals. Crystals also have very high vibrations, and there are specific crystals that are used by psychics in order to improve their psychic senses and channel energy in order to open up to the spirit world. Some ways that we can become attuned to spiritual energies and vibrations are to hold, carry, meditate, or sleep with crystals. Some of the types of crystals that exist are: high vibration crystals (clear, violet, indigo, and lighter colors) such as clear quartz, amethyst, selenite, or lapis lazuli. Grounding crystals (orange, red, black, and darker shades) such as black tourmaline, smoky quartz, jasper, and ruby.

Another way to become attuned with our psychic abilities is to utilize breathing meditations. Breathing is often referred to as the "life force," and so, it is important that we know how to properly breathe (through the diaphragm rather than through the chest). Breathing meditations enable us to delve deeply into our bodies, but also, to center ourselves and to feel more grounded.

Hemisync and binaural meditations are also types of meditations that can enhance psychic abilities. These can be described as sound waves that activate certain functions within the brain.

Assistance from spirits can enable us to reach higher realms of psychic consciousness as well. It is crucial, however, to ask for protection before opening ourselves up to any type of supernatural force. Certain meditations exist in order to meet our spirit guides. When we build relationships with these spirit guides, we will then come to know the ones that are able to help us with psychic development and other such areas.

Chapter Two: How to Have a Third Eye Awakening

For any type of psychic development, it is important to know how to open the third eye, given that the third eye enables us to see and to perceive the spiritual world more clearly. The third eye, much like possessing a sixth sense, is connected to our level of perception, awareness, and spiritual communication. It is also known as a chakra, being one of our 7 wheel-like energy centers that are spread throughout the body. The third eye chakra most heavily impacts the sense of well-being and perception. This particular chakra is thought to be located in the middle of our foreheads, and that, when opened, is linked with the qualities of wisdom, insight, and spiritual connection. There is no particular scientific evidence to back up these claims, but nevertheless, many cultures and traditions still believe in this phenomenon.

When it comes to having a third eye awakening, we must consider all the qualities that the third eye is associated with. Most commonly, the third eye is linked with the characteristics of: clarity, concentration, imagination, intuition, spiritual perception, and universal connection. This particular chakra is thought to be connected to the pineal gland, which is a pea-sized gland shaped like a pinecone, located in the vertebrate brain near the hypothalamus and pituitary gland.

In addition, the pineal gland is considered to be highly respected across many cultures, and to play quite a significant role. For example, in Ayurvedic philosophy, the third eye is represented by the Ajna chakra. In ancient Egypt, the symbol of the eye of Horus mirrors the placement of the pineal gland in the profile of the human head. The pineal gland is considered to be the physical or biological equivalent of the spiritual/energetic third eye chakra. This gland also emits the chemical of melatonin, which highly impacts circadian rhythms and reproductive hormones. Studies demonstrate a connection between the pineal gland and DMT (N, N-dimethyltriptamine), according to a 2019 research review. The chemical is, at times, referred to as "the spirit molecule" or "the seat of the soul" since it is so heavily linked to its relationship to consciousness.

If our third eye is blocked, then this could result in a tremendous amount of potential problems, though seemingly unapparent at first. These include: confusion, uncertainty, lack of purpose, and cynicism. However, when the third eye is healthily opened, this results in mental clarity, improved concentration, clear self-expression, strengthened intuition, a sense of bliss, decisiveness, and insight.

The third eye has been a topic of paramount discussion in the field of parapsychology, which is the study of unexplainable mental phenomena. Some individuals believe that, when the third eye is open, it behaves as a direct doorway for spiritual communication. Spiritual communication can include telepathy, clairvoyance, lucid dreaming, astral projection, and aura perception

There are many conflicting ideas and beliefs regarding how to open the third eye. Certain cultures and traditions believe that it is important to open and to get in touch with all the other chakras before opening the third eye. In turn, this action will ground us, and enable us to experience the insights of higher consciousness.

In order to open the third eye, we could try the following tactics: activating the third eye; supplementing our diet; applying essential oils; sungazing; meditating and chanting; and using crystals.

One example of a way in which we can open our third eye chakras is through activation exercises. You can start by sending gratitude to your third eye for your innate intuitive abilities and your connection to nature that the third eye governs. Another way that we can open our third eye chakras is by changing our diets. Some foods to include in your diet are: raw cacao; goji berries; garlic; lemon; watermelon; star anise; honey; coconut oil; hemp seeds; cilantro; ginseng; and vitamin D3.

The application of essential oils is yet another way that we are able to open the third eye chakra. The specific oils that are most often recommended are jasmine, lemon, and sandalwood.

In addition, the practice of sungazing can enable us to enhance our spiritual connections and thus, allow one's third eye to open. It is a method of meditation that includes staring at the sun, usually at the sunrise or sunset, and boosts our mental clarity and energy. Gaze gently at the sun during the first few minutes of sunrise and last few minutes of sunset to help awaken your third eye.

With meditating and chanting, it has been proven that mantra chanting can help to create a sense of deep appreciation and inner peace. It can also help to open up the third eye chakra. Meditation activates the pineal gland through vibration and intention. Consider visualizing the pineal gland filling with energy as you meditate.

Using crystals can cause us to have a third eye awakening, in addition to possessing healing qualities. Use crystals and gemstones in the purple, indigo, and violet color palette. This color palette is closely associated with the third eye chakra. Some specific crystals that can be utilized for third eye activation are: amethyst, purple sapphire, purple violet tourmaline, rhodonite, and sodalite. Crystals can be situated between or above the brow during times of meditation.

While it can take a long while to activate the third eye, there is no specific time frame or time limit during which this event will occur. As a universal principle, "practice makes perfect." Try dedicating some time each day to awakening your third eye. You may choose to start with just one of the methods mentioned here, or you could try to combine several of them. All will contribute to the awakening of your third eye chakra. This process can take some time and dedication, so patience is key.

Chapter Three: The Art of Psychic Mediumship

In the world of the occult, and especially in the world of psychics, there are some individuals who are able to communicate with spirits—and particularly, with the deceased. These people are known as mediums. They typically commune with these types of spirits while in states of trances, and spiritualist mediums are the primary influence during séances. During any sort of séance, incorporeal voices are thought to speak, either directly or via the medium. The manifestation of an incorporeal spirit or of a particular part of a human body can take shape from a substance called ectoplasm that comes from the medium's body and then goes away by going back to its original source. At specific times, the medium, or the tangible object, can seem to float in mid-air by means of levitation.

While there is some overlap between being a psychic and being a medium, there are essential core differences between the two. Being psychic does not necessitate being a medium, but all mediums are psychics.

Psychics are able to "tune into" the energy of people or objects by feeling, seeing, or perceiving portions of others' past, present, or future. Psychics depend upon their senses of intuition in order to accumulate information regarding what is being read or communicated.

Mediums, on the other hand, go a bit deeper. They do what psychics do in that they also see into elements of the individuals' past, present, and future, but they additionally tune into the spirit energy that is around them. Mediums rely upon intangible energy that goes beyond themselves in order to discover information for the people they are doing the reading for. There are many different types of mediums, including mental mediums, intuitive mediums, spiritual mediums, and so on. They, at times, can communicate with spirit guides, angels, and the deceased via telepathy.

A medium is essentially someone who is able to communicate with souls on the other side.

There are many ways in which mediums are able to communicate with the deceased. Some choose to undergo a form of possession, acting as a vessel for those spirits needing a human form to communicate with this world. Some interact with spirits as clearly as they do with those on this physical plane.

During a mediumship reading, the medium in question will link with loved ones on the other side. Then the medium will perceive, through clairvoyance, the individual who is passing through in order to communicate. He or she will observe physical features, clothing, or any other evidence of the person who is coming through.

Another category of a reading that some individuals invest in is a 'spiritual soul assessment'. It is essentially a reading that tells us where our life journey desires to take us, on a soul-deep level, based upon our gifts and callings. In this kind of reading, we may discover any blockages that have been hindering us from achieving our fullest potential as well as the next best move for our life paths. This reading enables us to evolve and to become closer to fulfilling our life's potential, as well as giving us the specific steps that we are able to take in order to remain true to our life's purpose.

Chapter Four: The Energy of Reiki and Other Healing Modalities

While it is important, as previously mentioned, to distinguish the art of being psychic from other aspects of spirituality and its related phenomenon, there is some overlap between certain spiritual skills and abilities. For example, the subject of the energy of reiki and other healing modalities carry a great deal of weight in the psychic world, although it is not restricted to such.

When coming to understand reiki, it is important to note that the mind-body connection is naturally one that is innately harmonious. When the balance becomes dysfunctional in some way, illnesses can come about. One particular approach to reiki healing is known as Mind-Body Bridging, which looks to bring back a better connection between the mind and the physical body. This is based upon the idea that we are able to learn how to use our thoughts in order to positively impact the body's physical responses.

In the eyes of some reiki practitioners, the mind, body, and spirit all exist in isolation from one another, and therefore, operate independently from each other. Understanding this principle is crucial to coming to comprehend the true nature of reiki.

Reiki can be described as a holistic Japanese method for stress reduction, relaxation, and spiritual healing. It can also be a way of connecting with one's higher power and a way of tapping into psychic abilities. "Rei" means "higher knowledge, spiritual consciousness," and "ki" means "life energy". Reiki can overall be considered spiritually guided life energy. Whenever there is some sort of constriction with the flow of energy within our bodies or spirits, reiki strives to restore this.

Reiki is typically performed while lying down or in a massage chair, and hands are placed either on, or above the client's body. Patients are fully clothed, and depending upon what the patient is able to endure, he or she will choose an appropriate length of time for a session.

Anyone can utilize the healing power of reiki, and it does not interfere with any medications that are prescribed by doctors. People can use reiki in order to heal themselves as well, with the training of a reiki teacher/master. Typically, classes are taken, during which they learn various hand positions that are traditionally used.

Some common conditions that reiki aims to treat are: cancer, heart disease, anxiety, depression, chronic pain, infertility, neurodegenerative disorders, autism, Crohn's disease, fatigue syndromes, and so on.

In order to become a reiki practitioner, no previous training, education, or experience is required. During this process, an "attunement of energy" occurs, and is said to be a "powerful spiritual experience." The master is thought to transmit the attunement energy and healing methods into the student.

While reiki training can vary, most students learn about: the energies around the body, how to work with healing energy, and the ethics of working with clients. In order to prepare for the attunement, the student may fast for two to three days, focus on nature, or release negative emotions. There are three levels of mastery, and those who achieve the "Master" level are able to teach others, conduct distance healing, and so on.

As far as the psychic aspect of reiki is concerned, there are certain reiki practitioners who will choose to communicate with ascended masters, angels, and spirit guides. These types of practitioners typically ask their angels for advice or guidance regarding their clients before their arrival. These reiki masters may pull some angel or tarot cards beforehand, and willingly receive messages concerning their clients about whatever issue or concern is pressing. Then the clients can apply these messages to their reiki sessions on the table, as they receive the healing energy that is being transmitted from a higher source, to the reiki master, and then onto the client.

Chapter Five: Psychic Readings from a Divinatory Lens

Divination is yet another aspect of the psychic world that enables us to come to a further understanding of ourselves and the world around us. It can be defined as 'the practice of determining the hidden significance or cause of events, sometimes foretelling the future, by various natural, psychological, and other techniques'. Discoverable in both ancient and modern societies, divination is associated with horoscopes, astrology, crystal gazing, tarot cards, and the Ouija board.

According to the Roman culture and belief system, divination was associated with finding out the will of the gods. But today, scholars do not restrict the word to its root meaning. Divination is so much more than knowledge; it requires intuition, but exists merely as a tool to guide us along our paths, and should never be taken at face value. The practice of divination is, in some societies, actually something that many people use regularly, but usually not in order to determine the will of the gods. Divination is most frequently practiced in the modern Western world via horoscopic astrology, but other types were and still are equally significant in other cultures.

The practice of divination is typically linked with practical issues, but is not always achieved through ordinary, or natural, means. We are part of the natural world, but through divination, we are able to gather information that is part of the supernatural world. It can deal with a variety of topics, but usually, during a divinatory reading, questions are asked of the cards or other such medium, and the reader will reveal the answer via what the cards reveal. There are many methods, attitudes, and styles of various readers; some readers will be more serious, while others will be more casual in mood or in nature.

The nature of divination depends heavily upon the motives of the diviners in question. It is not adequate to say that the information sought after in the readings are meant to diminish uncertainty, place blame, or overcome unfortunate events. There are two main categories of divinatory readings, and they are: general information about the future, and certain information concerning the past as it relates to the future.

Typically, clients turn to the advice of diviners when they are uncertain of a specific course of action to take in their lives. They seek advice be it based on illness, drought, fear of death; when there is suspicion of malevolence, theft, or breach of faith; when dreams or other symptoms are disturbing, or the signs of the times seem bad. Divination takes these areas of concern into account and figures out how to solve them. The diviner usually behaves as one who reveals hidden fears or motives, as well as potential future outcomes. While interpretation of readings can at times be considered arbitrary, they have nevertheless been considered reliable resources for those who may need guidance.

There are many forms and types of divination, some more easily perceived than others. Inductive divination utilizes non-human means, whether artificial or natural, as signs that are able to be explicitly read. It seems that these types of signs and divinations are more authentic than that of others.

This particular method of divination involves gazing at the heavens, reading signs in the weather, and the movement of birds. Additionally, lightning was considered to be a discernible message that has been carried forth by the gods.

Augury, the act of interpreting omens, is a prime example of inductive divination. It can be defined as the attempt to discover divine will phenomena of animate nature. Inductive divination is also connected with the reading of artificial events, such as the movement of sacrificial smoke, the fall of an arrow shot upward, or the rolling of dice.

Interpretive divination utilizes nonhuman phenomena with human action, taking devices that are so complex, subtle, or fluid that the gifts of the diviner are needed in order to comprehend the meaning of the reading. Within this category, divination seems to become the most dramatic.

Interpretive divination is, in essence, the reading of portents, omens, or prodigies. To a scientific or logical individual, no event happens without a reason. But it does seem as if arbitrary or random events happen even in a structured world, and these events are also subject to interpretation. Manipulated events are one aspect of interpretive divination, but the less active types are based upon projection, introjection, and free association. Therefore, to some extent, they are linked to intuitive methods.

Pyromancy, which is divination by fire, is considered to be one of the more dramatic forms of divination. During this process, objects are thrown into the fire, and signs are interpreted based on how they burn. Hydromancy (divination by water), on the other hand, is typically far less dramatic. It involves reading reflections from a shallow surface, similar to the way that a crystal gazer would read, as well as reading the movements of floating objects, akin to what a tea leaf reader would do.

Other related practices include cleromancy (divination by lots) and geomancy (the casting of objects upon a map or figure drawn on the ground).

Intuitive divination typically relies less frequently upon artificiality, except when dramatic effect is needed. Diviners can, for instance, make it a point to use other voices, in the sense that they are able to speak through the mouth of other gods or spirits. They can, at times, be induced by drugs or by autokinetic (self-energized) methods, such as hand trembling. Intuitive divination is also associated with trances, oracular utterance, and spirit possession.

Chapter Six: The Psychic World from an Astrological Lens

Another type of divination that can be heavily linked to the psychic world is that of astrology. Essentially, astrology can be defined as a type of divination that involves the forecasting of earthly and human events through the observation and interpretation of the fixed stars, the Sun, the Moon, and the planets. True believers in astrology think that the impact of the planet and the stars on earthly matters permits them to both predict and to impact the fates of individuals, groups, and nations. In the past, astrology was highly regarded and revered as a science, but nowadays, it is thought to be in stark contrast to modern Western science.

Astrology is, in essence, a technique of predicting any sort of event based on the idea that the celestial bodies (in particular, the planets and the stars, also known as constellations) are able to dictate changes that are being made in the temporal world.

There is a specific role of the divine that is thought to play a part in astrological theory. But in some aspects of astrology, there is no exact science, and it can be changed dramatically by divine or human will.

The core objective of astrology is to notify the individual of information based upon the positions of the planets and the zodiacal signs at the moment of his or her conception. From this particular science, referred to as genethlialogy (casting nativities) came the foundational methods of astrology. The subdivisions of astrology include: general, cathartic, and interrogatory.

General astrology makes note of the movements between celestial moments (e.g., times of vernal equinoxes, eclipses, or planetary conjunctions) to the whole of humanity—including social groups and all the nations.

Cathartic astrology discovers whether or not a chosen moment in astrology supports the action behind it. In other words, it permits the individual to behave during times that are astrologically favorable and to therefore, avoid any failures that can be predicted or foreseen.

Interrogatory astrology offers answers to a client's questions based upon the way that the celestial bodies are situated when he or she asks them. This method is more divinatory in nature than the other forms of astrology, and so, is more based upon reading omens and the divine will.

At its core, astrology endorses the belief that, since we remain part of the story of the Universe, our moment of birth that has been recorded on the celestial clock is rather significant. The planets continue to move in conjunction with the "fixed in time" energies of our birth charts.

Astrology is considered to be an important tool for self-discovery. Although, at times, life seems to be a random series of occurrences or coincidences, it actually is a sign that things in life may happen for a reason, and that there is more purpose to our lives than we could possibly imagine. It can shed light on inner strengths as well as points that need to be improved upon. Astrology behaves as a method of understanding the self that never ceases to provide layers upon layers of insight, knowledge, and intuition.

The key to comprehending astrology is in knowing that there are various types of wisdom, and that astrology only covers one of them. There are three aspects to all birth charts: planet, sign, and house. A blending occurs within the realm of astrology that involves all three aspects. As we learn more about all three aspects, we will come to a much stronger understanding of what each life lesson holds for us, particularly what is within our specific birth charts.

In terms of the planets of astrology, there are three main individual aspects embedded within it: the sun, moon, and ascendant. Our sun sign can be understood as our "vitality," our yang energy, and our will. This is the way that we appear to the world; our moon sign can be thought of as our emotional states, how we react, and where we feel the most safe or secure; and the ascendant is essentially the way that we view or approach the world around us.

The energies and placements of the other planets during the moments of our birth matter as well. The following describes each of the planets and their energies in terms of astrological placements:

- Mercury: thinking, listening, learning.

- Venus: values, possessions, the relating process (what we want and how it is attracted).

- Jupiter: abundance, expansion, growth.

- Saturn: fear, restriction, discipline, structure, reality.

- Uranus: freedom, sudden change, upheaval, unusual, eccentric.

- Neptune: fantasy, imagination, creativity, escape, confusion, addictions.

- Pluto: transformation, power, change, regeneration.

Conversely, when it comes to our signs (which are also referred to as signs of the zodiac), there are many of them, all of which can be associated with our dates of birth and the energies surrounding them.

The following describes each sign of the zodiac as well as characteristics that are linked with each of them:

- Aries (March 21-April 20): willpower, impulsive, initiative, courage, energy, activity. Often rushes headlong into things.

- Taurus (April 21-May 20): sensual, pleasure-seeker, steadfast, focused, can be stubborn, strives for security.

- Gemini (May 21-June 20): witty, communicative, always on the go, takes pleasure in learning.

- Cancer (June 21-July 20): emotional, nurturing, seeks safety and closeness, a family person. Tends to withdraw when feeling threatened.

- Leo (July 21-August 20): glamour, generosity, proud and loyal, dramatic, confident, an organizer. Likes the center stage.

- Virgo (August 21-September 20): precise, analytical, does what is necessary, practical. Can be a bit critical.

- Libra (September 21-October 20): a sense of beauty and proportion, tactful, seeks balance and harmony. Can have difficulty making a decision.

- Scorpio (October 21-November 20): passionate, piercing, extreme situations, transformation. The detectives of the zodiac.

- Sagittarius (November 21-December 20): free spirit, carefree, love of movement, cheerful, sees "the big picture."

- Capricorn (December 21-January 20): enduring, has a sense of purpose, proud, ambitious. Can get stuck in perfectionism.

- Aquarius (January 21-February 20): friendly, humanitarian, progressive, unconventional. Can seem emotionally detached.

- Pisces (February 21-March 20): sensitive, compassionate, helpful, sociable, adaptable. \

Similarly, the final aspect of astrology is the houses, each of which represent an angle of human life. There are twelve houses, and every one of them is linked with a zodiac sign and its corresponding planet.

The following houses exist as significant parts of astrology, and blend together with the zodiac as well as the state of the planets:

- 1st House (Ascendant)/Aries/Mars—the individual personality. Blended together with the sun and the moon signs, the ascendant is the most crucial aspect in a horoscope. The sign toward the beginning of the first house signifies a great deal about one's personality and disposition. It paints a solid picture of our intuitive reactions and demonstrates how we show ourselves to the world around us. This particular planet turns into the "ruler" of our astrological charts.

- 2nd House/Taurus/Venus—values and possessions. The second house signifies our circumstances as well as how we handle our material goods. It is a house of values, and thus, will indicate the ways in which we value or treat ourselves. Problems of self-worth may come about in this particular house.

- 3rd House/Gemini/Mercury—communication. The third house shows the way that we speak or communicate on a daily basis, the way that we learn at school, and the relationships that we form within our local communities.

- 4th House/Cancer/Moon—roots and origins. This house explains our roots and origins, the house in which we were raised, and the circumstances that impacted our childhood. It explains how we relate to family, and our dispositions toward hearth and home. It especially focuses on the image of the relationship to one's father.

- 5th House/Leo/Sun –pleasure and creativity. This is the house of creative expression, whether it is through the arts, the kitchen, the garage, or through childbearing. This particular house is occupied with a parent's feelings toward his or her children. It is the house of playful love affairs rather than strong, committed love.

- 6th House/Virgo/Mercury—work and routine. This house demonstrates how we are able to handle our daily work and routine. It signifies how disciplined we are when challenged with routine, whether chained to it, or highly disorganized in nature. It is also related to issues of health and diet.

- 7th House/Libra/Venus—relating. This descendant sign and planets that reside within the seventh house signify how we are able to pick our partners and describe the partnerships that we most strongly seek. Usually, we are most strongly attracted to those whose horoscopes have an emphasis in the seventh house.

- 8th House/Scorpio/Pluto—loss and common property. The eighth house demonstrates exactly how we respond to communal possessions and physical loss. In traditional astrology, this house is related to death or anything beyond this realm. It also has connotations with darker things and the study of metaphysics.

- 10th House (MC)/Capricorn/Saturn—occupation and calling. This house impacts our personal professions and callings in our lives, but also, our development as individuals, which will be continuous.

- 11th House/Aquarius/Uranus—friends and acquaintances. The eleventh house explains exactly how we relate to friends and acquaintances, as well as those in positions of authority—in other words, those from whom we can learn significantly. It demonstrates our roles in society, as well as our personal goals and aspirations.

- 12th House/Pisces/Neptune—beyond the personal. This house deals with both escapism and isolation, as well as mystery and the unconscious mind. A sense of sacrifice is connected with this house, but it is the type that is linked with inner strength.

Chapter Seven: Automatic Writing and its Modern Uses

Automatic writing, which is the process or product of writing without using the conscious mind, is a method that is frequently utilized while the writer is caught within a trance-like state. Some who use this method, however, are completely awake and cognizant of their environment, but not the actions of their writing hands. Automatic writing, a key component of the Spiritualist and New Age movements, is a technique that also involves the "channeling" of spirits and has frequently occurred in séances. Throughout the Surrealist movement, automatic writing was a game that was played by artists in order to ignite creativity and to help them to come up with original works of art. Additionally, automatic writing has been used as a therapeutic method in Freudian psychoanalysis. During an automatic writing session, mediums typically channel spirits, permitting them to guide the pencils or planchettes, and then coming up with messages that the spirits desired to speak to the world of the living. While channeling permits the spirit to take advantage of the medium's body in order to communicate, possession is much different, in that it is involuntary.

There are many steps involved in successfully practicing automatic writing. One of them is to avoid all possible distractions. We cannot connect well with the inner self or the metaphysical world if we have things around us that are distracting us. It is crucial for us to leave behind any earthly concerns and to concentrate on our subconscious minds in order to establish a deeper link with our higher selves.

Then we should pick a particular spiritual being when we begin. This works well for one who has just begun to establish psychic ability. It is advisable to begin with writing down names on pieces of paper or to simply call out spirits by their names. Nevertheless, it is crucial to continue to consider the spirit throughout the process and to keep our auras open to them.

After this, we ought to work with a clear mind. It will take a great deal of time and effort in order to get to the proper state of mind and for the automatic writing to truly work. No matter what we do, our minds are constantly thinking. It is important to practice the skill of tuning out analytical thought and instead concentrate solely on supernatural forces. If we allow these forces to take control of things, then we will be in a better state to let automatic writing work for us. A strong way of taking more control over our thought processes is to practice meditation. It enables us to clear our minds and helps us to become aligned with our spiritual centers.

There are many positive aspects to automatic writing. Some of them are:

- You gain direct guidance from your Soul/Higher Self
- You'll have more clarity in your daily life as a result
- Improved ability to make wise decisions
- Your intuitive abilities are sharpened, honed, and developed
- You can connect with your Spirit Guides and their perspectives
- You feel supported and deeply understood
- Improved ability to trust your instincts and intuition

In order to be successful in the practice of automatic writing, it is important that we take the following steps:

- Get a pen and paper/open a notepad or word document
- Think of a question to ask

The more emotional the question is, the more clarity that we will receive when obtaining an answer. It is also crucial that we direct our questions to someone or something specifically, such as our souls, a spirit guide, or our unconscious minds.

For instance, our question could be, "Dear soul, why do I keep compromising my own happiness?" For the clearest answers, it is best to keep the questions as simple as possible.

- Write down the question
- Interpret the information

Eventually, the session will come to an end. We will sense this through intuition sometimes, and other times, we might suddenly stop writing and no more information will come through.

Once we have ceased writing, it will be important to review what we have written, and to then search for coherent sentences or keywords that may stand out. At times, we will find patterns, and in some scenarios, words from other languages.

- Relax your body and mind

Learning how to relax your mind is one of the most crucial aspects of automatic writing. When our minds are quieted and devoid of thoughts, writing in the spur of the moment is made far easier.

Examples of potential ways that we can relax our minds include: meditation, deep breathing, mindfulness, visualization, and yoga

- Allow the writing to flow spontaneously

Once we are ready, we can start to write. Initially, we may not understand what the words are trying to convey, but even if we do not know what they are saying, this is a good sign, since it means that we are tapping into something that goes beyond ourselves.

It is also typical during this stage to judge and analyze what we are writing. If we find our minds getting involved, it is important for us to bring ourselves back to the practice that we utilized before we entered the trance-like state. For instance, if we were breathing rhythmically, we should go back to doing that.

Before beginning an automatic writing session, it is important to give ourselves enough time to convey what needs to be conveyed. One certain way to stop the flow of information is time pressure and the unrealistic expectation that it should take a specific amount of time. Automatic writing can take from two minutes to an hour.

- Enter a gentle trance.

A trance-like state is essentially a state of altered consciousness within the brain during which our "normal brain" relaxes. For automatic writing, getting into a trance is especially useful because it brings forth the spontaneous flow of information.

The most common ways to get into a trance-like state include listening to music, yogic/holotropic breathing, mantras, repetitive tasks, guided meditations, self-hypnosis, and so on.

Automatic writing is, however, a skill that we need to develop with both patience and practice, unless we have a natural knack for it.

Chapter Eight: Healing Crystals and Colored Stones

There are many modern-day uses for crystals and colored stones, particularly within New Age circles. Each crystal possesses its own unique healing powers and energies. The following are examples of crystals that are commonly used:

- White/Clear crystal: clear quartz, selenite, apophyllite, white chalcedony, and moonstone.

White crystals are all utilized for cleansing and purification purposes. Clear quartz, for instance, is commonly used for its power to amplify the energy of other crystals, and selenite is often considered cleansing for any space. Crystals that are clear/white are typically easy to connect with and are good for promoting peace and tranquility. They are very good to use during meditations or for energy work.

- Red crystals: red jasper, ruby, vanadinite, garnet, rubellite.

This crystal type is all about getting energized and taking charge. They get us feeling "pumped up," passionate, and ready to take action. These are the most highly intense and raw in energy.

- Pink crystals: rose quartz, rhodochrosite, pink tourmaline, rhodonite, pink opal.

This type of crystal motivates us to be warm, loving, and compassionate within our hearts. Gentle and emotionally healing, pink is good for bringing more love and kindness into our lives. It is crucial to meditate on or carry pink crystals when dealing with matters of the heart, such as forgiveness, romance, self-love, or love for others.

- Orange crystals: sunstone, carnelian, orange calcite, sunset aura quartz, amber.

This crystal type is connected to any creative activity, enthusiasm, or sexuality. They can bring forth creative inspiration, whether it is used for an art project or in the bedroom. These crystals also are helpful when it comes to reflecting on major transformations in life. When it comes to major decisions or choices in life, this crystal can be of good use.

- Yellow crystals: citrine, golden onyx, honey calcite, yellow jasper, sulfur quartz.

Yellow crystals are all about self-expression, as well as being bright, sunny, and optimistic toward life. They are able to bring forth positive energy into any given situation and help to support others in being their true, authentic selves. Yellow crystals can additionally make our beliefs about self-empowerment much stronger, so they are able to make us feel more confident.

- Green crystals: malachite, jade, peridot, moss agate, green aventurine.

Green, being the color of both plants and money, is most frequently used for manifesting abundance, wealth, and fortune, and to support our growth, whether that is a spiritual, emotional, or economical type of growth. Green is also the color of connecting with nature and with the earth's energy.

- Blue crystals: lapis lazuli, aquamarine, blue lace agate, larimar, azurite.

Blue crystals can be very soft, tranquil, and serene. They can calm our emotions, but they are also quite powerful. They signify clarity of communication and honesty of self-expression. Blues bring forth clarity and strength when it comes to speaking truthfully, boldly, and honestly with ourselves and with others.

- Purple crystals: amethyst, lepidolite, spirit quartz, charoite, sugilite.

Purple crystals are about spiritual energy and intuition. They enable us to become more connected with the mystical aspects of ourselves, as well as our higher selves. Purples can help us to become more in tune with the divine spiritual realm, creativity, or spirituality in general.

- Black crystals: obsidian, black tourmaline, shungite, jet, black kyanite.

These crystals get rid of all negativity and fear. They also ignite a strong sense of physical and emotional security. Often used as a "shield" against negative auras/vibes, they are useful for dealing with distressing situations

Chapter Nine: Divination Continued: Tarot Card Reading

Within the psychic world and among various faith traditions, the practice of divination is commonly utilized to either be predictive or provide insight regarding present situations. They also can be reflective in nature, igniting feelings of wisdom concerning internal struggles.

One particular form of divination that is widely used today is the tarot. Often misunderstood and feared by outsiders who are unfamiliar with its true nature, there are many aspects of tarot that can actually be utilized positively, and do not need to be predictive at the core.

The history of the tarot is rather complex. Dated from the 15th century and utilized in many parts of Europe, it was originally used as a pack of cards to play games such as Italian tarocchini, French tarot, and Austrian Konigrufen, which are still played to this day.

In the late 18th century, some of the tarot decks started to be used for divinatory purposes as well as cartomancy, ultimately leading to decks that were specifically designed for the world of the occult.

Similar to regular playing cards, tarot has four suits: Wands, Cups, Swords, and Pentacles. Each suit contains 14 cards: ten pip cards numbered from one (Ace) to ten, and four face cards (King, Queen, Knight, and Jack/Knave/Page). The tarot deck also has a separate 21-card trump suit and a single card that is known as the Fool. This particular part of the tarot deck is known as the Major Arcana. Depending upon the game that is being played, the Fool may act as the top trump or not. The tarot cards are, to this day, still utilized throughout Europe in order to play ordinary card games without any occult links.

Within many English-speaking countries where these types of games are not played often, and tarot cards are mainly used for divinatory means, typically using specially designed packs. Some who use tarot for cartomancy think that the cards have links to ancient Egypt, the Kabbalah, Indian Tantra, or the I Ching, although research cannot confirm nor deny this.

In terms of occult usage, Etteilla (Jean-Baptiste Alliette), was the first to distribute a tarot deck that was especially designed for these purposes around the year 1789. Since Etteilla desired to stay in line with the belief that cards came from the Book of Thoth, Etteilla's tarot held themes that were relevant to ancient Egypt.

The 78-card tarot deck that was used by esotericists contained two major parts:

- The Major Arcana (greater secrets), or trump cards, which contains 22 cards without suits: The Magician, The High Priestess, The Empress, The Emperor, The Hierophant, The Lovers, The Chariot, Strength, The Hermit, Wheel of Fortune, Justice, The Hanged Man, Death, Temperance, The Devil, The Tower, The Star, The Moon, The Sun, Judgement, The World, and The Fool. Cards from The Magician to The World are numbered in Roman numerals from I to XXI, and the Fool is the only unnumbered card, at times placed at the beginning as 0, or at the end as XXII.

- The Minor Arcana (lesser secrets) contains 56 cards, divided into 4 suits of 14 cards each: Ten numbered cards and four court cards. The cards are the King, the Queen, Knight, and Page/Jack, in each of the four tarot suits. The traditional Italian tarot suits are swords, batons, coins, and cups. In modern occult decks, the batons are referred to as wands, rods, or staves, while the coins are called pentacles or disks.

Some decks exist primarily for the artwork, while others have only the 22 Major Arcana. The three most common decks that are used are the

Tarot of Marseilles, the Rider-Waite-Smith tarot deck, and the Thoth tarot deck.

Aleister Crowley, who constructed the Thoth deck along with Lady Frieda Harris, says of the tarot, "The origin of this pack of cards is very obscure. Some authorities seek to put it back as far as the ancient Egyptian Mysteries; others try to bring it forward as late as the fifteenth or even the sixteenth century ... [but] The only theory of ultimate interest about the Tarot is that it is an admirable symbolic picture of the Universe, based on the data of the Holy Qabalah."

There are many different meanings of tarot cards. Although each card meaning is specific to individual situations, there are general meanings that apply to each of the cards themselves. They have both upright and reversed meanings.

When receiving a reading, or conducting a reading on oneself, the cards should be shuffled, and the meanings received thereafter.

The following can be described as common meanings for each of the cards, depending upon whether the cards are drawn upright, or upside down, which we call reversed:

- **The Fool.** Upright: beginnings, innocence, spontaneity, a free spirit.

Reversed: holding back, recklessness, risk-taking.

The fool can exist either at the beginning or end of one's life journey, and therefore, does not need a number because he always exists. On the Fool card, a young man stands on the edge of a cliff, feeling very carefree as he sets out on new adventures. He is observing the sky upward and seems to be unaware that he is about to head off into unknown territory. On his shoulder, he straps a knapsack that has all his necessities, which is not that much. The white rose in his left hand signifies purity and innocence; at his feet is a small white dog, which symbolizes loyalty and protection and motivates him to move forward and learn the lessons he is meant to. The mountains that are behind the Fool represent the challenges that are to come, which are always there, but the Fool doesn't seem to care about them for the time being because he is more focused on starting over.

- **The Magician.** Upright: Manifestation, resourcefulness, power, inspired action.

Reversed: Manipulation, poor planning, untapped talents.

The Magician card is the number one, which signifies new beginnings and opportunities, and is linked with the planet Mercury. He stands with one arm stretched up toward the universe, and the other pointing down to the earth. The way that he is positioned signifies his link between the spiritual realms and the material realms. The Magician uses this relationship to manifest his objectives in material reality. He is the source that creates energy into matter. His robe is white, which signifies purity, and his cloak is red, which symbolizes worldly knowledge and experience.

On the table in front of him stand the four symbols of the Tarot suits—a cup, pentacle, sword, and wand—all of which stand for one of the four elements—water, earth, air, or fire. This also signifies that he possesses all the tools that are required in order to manifest his desires into reality. Above his head is the infinity symbol, and around his waist is a snake that is biting its own tail, both of which signify that he has limitless access to untapped potential. In the foreground there are a great deal of flowers, which stand for the blossoming of his own ideas and goals.

- **The High Priestess.** Upright: Intuition, sacred knowledge, divine feminine, the subconscious mind.

Reversed: Secrets, disconnection from intuition, withdrawal, and silence.

The High Priestess, in this card, is sitting in front of a thin veil that is adorned with pomegranates. The veil signifies the separation between the conscious and subconscious mind, the seen and the unseen realms, and behaves as a way of keeping casual onlookers out. Only "the initiated" are permitted to enter. The pomegranates on the veil are symbols of abundance, fertility, and the divine feminine, and remain sacred to Persephone, who in Greek mythology consumed a pomegranate seed in the underworld and was made to return every year.

On each side of the High Priestess are two pillars, marking the entrance to this sacred, mystical temple, which is also connected with the Temple of Solomon. One pillar is black with the letter B (Boaz, meaning "in his strength"), and the other is white with the letter J (Jachin, meaning "he will establish"). The black and white pigments of the pillars represent duality—masculine and feminine, darkness and light—suggesting that knowledge and acceptance of duality are needed in order to enter this holy space.

The High Priestess is adorned in a blue robe with a cross on her chest and a horned diadem (crown), a symbol of both her divine knowledge and status as a divine ruler. In her lap, she carries a scroll with the letters TORA, suggesting the Greater Law. It is partly covered, suggesting that this sacred knowledge is both implicit and explicit, and that it will be unveiled when the student is willing to go beyond this material world. The crescent moon at her feet symbolizes her connection with the divine feminine, her intuition and subconscious mind, the natural moon cycles.

- **The Empress.** Upright: Femininity, beauty, nature, nurturing, abundance.

Reversed: Creative block, dependence on others.

The Empress is a beautiful, full-figured woman with blonde hair and a tranquil aura. She adorns a crown on her head that contains twelve stars, demonstrating her connection with the mystical realm as well as the cycles of the natural world (the twelve months of the year and the twelve planets). Her robe has patterns with pomegranates, which symbolizes fertility, and sits upon a luxurious set of cushions and flowing red velvet. One cushion holds the symbol of Venus, which is the planet of love, creativity, fertility, beauty, and grace—also the heart of the Empress.

A beautiful, luscious forest and winding stream surround the Empress, suggesting her link with Mother Earth and life as a whole. She takes her sense of serenity from the trees and the water and is replenished by the energy of nature. In the foreground, golden wheat grows out of the soil, which reflects abundance from a recent harvest.

- **The Emperor.** Upright: Authority, establishment, structure, a father figure.

Reversed: Domination, excessive control, lack of discipline, inflexibility.

The Emperor is the Father archetype of the Tarot deck, much like the Empress is the Mother archetype. He is seated upon a large stone throne, with four rams' heads (symbolic of his connection with Aries and the planet Mars). In his right hand, the Emperor possesses an ankh, the Egyptian symbol of life, and in his left, he holds an orb, which symbolizes the world over which he rules.

He wears a red robe, which suggests his power, passion, and zeal for life. Beneath it, he wears a suit of armor, which means that he is protected from any threat (or any other emotional response or vulnerability). His long white beard symbolizes his wisdom and experience, and with his golden crown, he is an authority figure who demands to be heard.

Behind his throne stands a tall mountain range, which suggests that he has a solid foundation, and doesn't make any changes until he believes it is completely necessary. Beneath the peaks lies a small river, providing some hope that in spite of his rigid exterior, he is still quite emotional—it will simply take some deep digging and trust to get him to open up and demonstrate that he has a softer side.

- **The Hierophant.** Upright: Spiritual wisdom, religious beliefs, conformity, tradition, institutions.

Reversed: Personal beliefs, freedom, challenging the status quo.

The Hierophant acts as the masculine counterpart to the High Priestess. In some Tarot decks, he is referred to as the Pope or the Teacher and is ruled by Taurus.

The Hierophant is a religious individual who sits between two pillars of a holy temple, although this particular temple is different from the one upon which the High Priestess sits. He wears three robes (red, blue, and white) and a three-tiered crown (the conscious, subconscious, and superconscious). He carries a Papal Cross in his left hand, a triple wand that symbolizes his religious status. He raises his right hand to give a religious blessing, with two fingers that point toward Heaven and two that point down toward Earth.

Two followers kneel down before him. The Hierophant's mission is primarily to pass on his spiritual wisdom and initiate the two followers into the church so that they can take up their designated roles. This image refers to a shared group identity and a rite of passage to move on to the next level. The cross keys at the Hierophant's feet signify the balance between the subconscious and conscious minds and the unveiling of mysteries, which only he can teach.

- **The Lovers.** Upright: Love, harmony, relationships, values alignment, choices.

Reversed: Self-love, disharmony, imbalance, misalignment of values.

The Lovers card demonstrates a naked man and woman who are standing beneath an angel, Raphael, whose name means "God heals" and signifies both physical and emotional healing. The angel blesses the man and the woman and brings to mind their connection with the Divine.

The man and woman stand within a beautiful, fertile landscape, which reminds one of the Garden of Eden. Behind the woman is a tall apple tree, with a snake that is crawling up the trunk. The snake and the apple tree symbolize the temptation of sexual pleasures that may take one's focus off the Divine. Behind the man is a tree of flames, which portray passion, the main concern of the man. The twelve flames signify the twelve zodiac signs, the ultimate symbol of time and eternity. The man looks over toward the woman, who observes the angel, conveying the path of the conscious to the subconscious to the super-conscious, or from physical desire to emotional needs to spiritual concerns.

The volcanic mountain in the background conveys an explosion of passion, and is quite sexual in nature, which occurs when man and woman meet in naked form.

- **The Chariot.** Upright: control, willpower, success, action, determination.

Reversed: self-discipline, opposition, lack of direction.

The Chariot card conveys a courageous warrior standing inside a chariot. He is adorned with armor that is decorated with crescent moons (which conveys what comes into being), a tunic with a square (the strength of will), and other alchemical symbols (spiritual transformation). The laurel and star crown symbolize victory, success, and spiritual evolution. Though he seems to be driving the chariot for himself, the charioteer carries no reins—simply a wand like the Magician's—representing that he controls through the strength and will of his mind.

The charioteer stands tall, given that he is in favor of taking action and moving forward from there. Above his head is a canopy of six-pointed stars, which represents his link to the ethereal realms and the Divine will. In front of the chariot is a black and white sphinx, which symbolizes duality, positive and negative, and sometimes conflicting forces. The sphinxes are pulling at each other in opposing directions, but the charioteer utilizes his willpower and inner strength in order to propel the chariot forward toward the direction he desires.

Behind the chariot is a wide river, which represents the need to "be in the flow" with the rhythm of life while also moving swiftly ahead toward our goals and objectives.

- **The Strength.** Upright: strength, courage, persuasion, influence, compassion.

Reversed: self-doubt, low energy, raw emotion.

In the Strength card, a woman softly caresses a lion on its forehead and mouth. Although it is renowned for its ferocity, the woman has tamed this wild lion with her peaceful, compassionate energy. The lion is symbolic of raw passions and desires, and the woman demonstrates that animal instinct and raw passion can be shown in beneficial ways when inner strength and tenacity are utilized. She does not use forcefulness of any kind, but channels her inner strength to calm and subtly influence the lion.

The woman is adorned in a white robe, demonstrating her pure spirit, and a belt and crown of flowers that signify the most complete and beautiful expression of nature. Over her head is the infinity symbol, which conveys her infinite potential and wisdom.

- **The Hermit.** Upright: soul-searching, introspection, being alone, inner guidance.

Reversed: isolation, withdrawal, loneliness.

The Hermit stands entirely alone at the top of a mountain. The snow-capped mountain range demonstrates his spiritual astuteness and mastery, personal growth, and success. He has decided on this path of self-fulfillment and self-discovery, and as a result, he has achieved a heightened state of awareness.

In his right hand, he carries a lantern with a six-pointed star inside, which is the Seal of Solomon, a seal of wisdom. As the Hermit walks down his path, the lamp lights his way, but it only shows his next few steps as opposed to the entire journey. He must move forward in order to observe where to go next, fully aware that not everything will be shown all at one time. In his left hand, the side of the subconscious mind, the Hermit carries a long rod (a symbol of his power and authority), which he uses to guide and keep him in balance.

- **Wheel of Fortune.** Upright: good luck, karma, life cycles, destiny, a turning point.

Reversed: bad luck, resistance to change, breaking cycles.

The Wheel of Fortune card displays a giant wheel, with three figures on the outer edges. Four Hebrew letters—YHVH (Yod Heh Vau Heh), the unpronounced name of God—are etched on the wheel's face. There are also the letters TORA, considered to be a version of the word "Torah," meaning "law," or "Tarot," even "ROTA" (Latin for "wheel"). The middle wheel possesses the alchemical symbols for mercury, sulfur, water, and salt—the building blocks of life and the four elements—and stands for formative power.

A serpent is on the outside, the Egyptian god Typhon (the god of evil) descending from the left side. The serpent also signifies life force energy that goes down into the material world. On the right side, the god Anubis comes up, the Egyptian god of the dead who introduces souls to the Underworld. On top of the wheel is the Sphinx, which signifies knowledge and strength.

In the corners of the Wheel of Fortune card stand four winged creatures, every one of them connected with the four fixed signs of the zodiac: the angel is Aquarius, the eagle is Scorpio, the lion is Leo, and the bull is Taurus. Their wings stand for stability in the middle of movement and transformation, and each of them carries the Torah, which holds wisdom.

- **Justice.** Upright: justice, fairness, truth, cause and effect, law.

Reversed: unfairness, lack of accountability, dishonesty.

The image of Justice sits in front of a loosely hung purple veil, representing mercy, and between two pillars, akin to those framing the

High Priestess and the Hierophant, which stand for balance, structure, and law.

She holds a sword in her right hand, demonstrating the rational, well-ordered mindset that is required in order to give out justice. The sword goes upward, marking a firm and rigid choice, and the double-edged blade shows that our actions always bear consequences. The scales in her left hand, which represents intuition, demonstrates that intuition must be balanced with logic, and exists as a symbol of her lack of partiality. Justice is wearing a crown with a small square on it that signifies well-ordered thoughts, and a red robe with a green mantle. A little white shoe pops out from underneath her clothing as a reminder that there are spiritual consequences to our actions.

- **The Hanged Man.** Upright: pause, surrender, letting go, new perspectives.

Reversed: delays, resistance, stalling, indecision.

The Hanged Man displays a man who is suspended from a T-shaped cross that is composed of living wood. He is hanging upside-down, observing the world from an entirely new point of view, and his face is tranquil, suggesting that he is in this hanging position by his own making. He has a halo around his head, signifying new insight, awareness, and enlightenment. His right foot is connected to the tree, but his left foot is loose, bent at the knee and tucked in behind his right leg. His arms are bent, with hands behind his back, making an inverted triangle. The man is wearing red pants, which symbolizes human passion and the human body. The Hanged Man is a quest for ultimate surrender, of being suspended in time, and of martyrdom and sacrifice to the greater good.

- **Death.** Upright: endings, change, transformation, transition.

Reversed: resistance to change, personal transformation, inner purging.

The Death card illustrates the Messenger of Death—a skeleton that is dressed in black, riding a black horse. The skeleton symbolizes the part of the body that survives long after life has left it; the armor signifies invincibility, and that death comes no matter what. The dark color is one of mourning, sorrow, and the mysterious, whereas the horse is the symbol of purity and acts as a symbol of strength and power. Death possesses a black flag that is adorned with a white, five-petal rose, which represents beauty, purification, and immortality, whereas the number five suggests transformation. Both of these symbols together suggest that death is not merely about the end of life. Death is about both endings and beginnings, birth and rebirth, change and transformation. There is a certain type of beauty that can be found in death, and it is a part of being truly alive.

A royal figure seems to be dead on the ground, whereas a young woman, child, and bishop beg with the skeletal figure to save their lives. But alas, death is inevitable.

In the background, a boat flows down the river, similar to the mythological boats that take the dead to the afterlife. On the horizon, the sun sets between two towers (which also manifest in the Moon Tarot card). So, in a sense, they are dying each night, and being reborn every morning.

- **Temperance.** Upright: balance, moderation, patience, purpose.

Reversed: imbalance, excess, self-healing, realignment.

The Temperance card conveys a large, winged angel who carries both masculine and feminine traits. She is adorned in a light blue robe with a triangle that is enclosed in a square on the front, demonstrating that humans (the triangle) are bound by the Earth and natural law (square). The angel balances with one foot on the rocks, portraying the requirement to stay grounded, and one foot in the water, conveying the need to be in flow. She pours water between two cups, which symbolizes the alchemy and flow of life.

In the background, there is a winding path up the mountain range, conveying the journey through life. Above the mountains hovers a golden crown encased in a glowing light, which represents taking the Higher path in life, and remaining true to one's life purpose, goals, and meaning.

- **The Devil.** Upright: shadow self, attachment, addiction, restriction, sexuality.

Reversed: releasing limiting beliefs, exploring dark thoughts, detachment.

The Devil card demonstrates Baphomet, or the Horned Goat of Mendes, which is a creature that is partly man and partly goat. Baphomet initially signified the balance between good and evil, male and female, and human and animal. Most recently, however, the creature has been connected with the occult and has turned into the scapegoat for all things coined as "evil."

The Devil possesses the wings of a vampire bat, a creature that sucks the lifeblood out of its prey, which signifies what happens when we relent to our raw desires. He possesses a hypnotic gaze and captivates those who get close to him, bringing them under his power. An inverted pentagram is above him, which is a sign of the darker side of magic and occultism. He raises his right hand in the Vulcan Salute, which is a Jewish blessing. He carries a torch in his left hand.

A man and a woman are at the feet of the Devil, both naked and chained to the podium upon which the Devil sits. The man and woman seem to be held there against their will, but if one takes a closer glimpse, the chains can be easily taken off. Each of them has small horns on their heads, similar to the devil's, which is a symbol that they are becoming more like him the longer that they remain there. Both possess tails, which is a huge symbol of their animalistic habits and raw instincts, and the grapes and the fire on their tails convey lustful pleasure.

- **The Tower.** Upright: sudden change, upheaval, chaos, revelation, awakening.

Reversed: personal transformation, fear of change, averting disaster.

The Tower card displays a tall tower that sits atop a rocky mountain. Lightning strikes the building, and two people leap from the windows, head first and arms reaching outward. It is a place of chaos and destruction.

The Tower is a solid structure, but because it has been constructed on shaky foundations, it only takes one bolt of lightning to strike it down. It signifies ambitions and objectives that have been built upon false promises.

The lightning symbolizes a sudden surge of energy and insight that leads to a sudden breakthrough or revelation. It enters through the top of a building and knocks off the crown, which represents energy that flows down from the Universe, through the crown chakra. All the people are dying to escape from the burning building, unaware of what awaits them as they fall. Surrounding them are 22 flames, signifying the 12 signs of the zodiac and 10 points of the Tree of Life, meaning that even during disastrous times, there is always hope for divine intervention.

- **The Star.** Upright: hope, faith, purpose, renewal, spirituality.

Reversed: lack of faith, despair, self-trust, disconnection.

The Star conveys a naked woman who is kneeling toward the edge of a small pool. She possesses two containers of water: one in her left hand (the subconscious) and one in her right (the conscious). She pours out the water to replenish the earth and to continue the cycle of fertility, which is symbolized by the luscious greenery that surrounds her. The other container pours the water onto dry land in five rivulets, which stand for each of the five senses.

The woman has one foot on the ground, which stands for her practical capabilities, and strong common sense, while the other foot stands in the water, symbolizing her intuition and inner resources, or listening to her own inner voice. She is completely nude, which symbolizes her vulnerability and purity beneath the complete vastness of the starry sky. Behind her, one star is shining, which stands for the core of who she is, and there are seven smaller stars, which represent the seven chakras.

- **The Moon.** Upright: illusion, fear, anxiety, subconscious, intuition.

Reversed: release of fear, repressed emotion, inner confusion.

The Moon card depicts a full moon in the night's sky, held between two enormous towers. The Moon stands for intuition, dreams, and the unconscious state of mind. The light is waning in comparison to the sun, and just barely reflects the path to higher consciousness that winds between the two towers.

In the foreground is a small pool, which signifies the watery nature of the subconscious mind. A tiny crayfish crawls out of the pool, which represents the early stages of the consciousness to unfold. A dog and a wolf stand in the grassy field, which represent both the wild and tamed facets of our minds.

- **The Sun.** Upright: positivity, fun, joy, success, vitality.

Reversed: inner child, feeling down, overly optimistic.

The Sun card reflects nothing but sheer warmth, optimism, and positivity. A large, bright orb of a sun shines in the sky, which reflects the life source of all the Earth. Beneath it, four sunflowers are growing tall above a brick wall, which symbolize the four suits of the Minor Arcana and the four elements.

In the foreground, there is a young, nude child who is sitting atop a serene, white horse. The child depicts the joy and happiness of connection with our inner spirits, and his nakedness serves as a reminder that he does not have anything to hide and that he has all the innocence and purity of his childhood. The white horse additionally symbolizes purity and strength.

- **Judgement.** Upright: judgement, rebirth, inner calling, absolution.

Reversed: self-doubt, inner critic, ignoring the call.

The Judgement card depicts nude men, women, and children who are rising from their graves, arms outstretched and looking up into the sky. Above, Archangel Gabriel—the Messenger of God—sounds his trumpet. Everyone responds to his call, accepting judgment, to find out whether they will be accepted into heaven or not. A mountain range is in the background, which symbolizes the obstacles and inevitability of avoiding judgment.

- **The World.** Upright: completion, integration, accomplishment, travel.

Reversed: seeking personal closure, short-cuts, delays.

The World card depicts a nude woman who is wrapped in a purple cloth, dancing inside a large laurel wreath. She looks behind her toward her past, as her body moves forward in the opposite direction to the future. She holds two wands or batons in her hands, just like the one that the Magician holds. This symbolizes the fact that the World has completed what the Magician has begun. The wreath is circular, which stands for a constant cycle of completion and new beginnings since, as the woman steps through the wreath, she is completing one phase but starting another one almost immediately.

Surrounding the wreath stand four figures (a lion, bull, cherub, and eagle), which are similar to those found in the Wheel of Fortune. Both the World and the Wheel of Fortune signify the cyclical nature of life and the way that we progress through life. The four figures stand for the four fixed signs of the zodiac—Leo, Taurus, Aquarius, and Scorpio. They signify the four elements, the four suits of the Tarot, four compass points, four seasons, and the four corners of the Universe. They exist in order to guide us from one phase to the next, bringing ultimate balance and harmony to our journeys.

Final Words

Although there are various ways in which we can tap into our psychic abilities, many still choose to disbelieve in the power and authority of these methods. There exist many techniques to tap into the psychic realm, although it takes much time and effort to develop these abilities.

In spite of the fact that science and culture tend to question the nature of the psychic world, it is important for us to be aware and to remain in tune with our spiritual selves if we so desire to open ourselves up to that realm. Science and spirituality as disciplines may seem to conflict with one another, but it seems as though, in some instances, they remain in harmony, and this is when our true psychic abilities tend to open up.

The psychic realm can refer to many subcategories, and one of them is mediumship. If we would like to become mediums, then we must first become truly psychic. Mediumship is characterized by the ability to communicate with the dead in order to gain insight about this current world, while being psychic can be more closely related to the human soul or mind, meaning that he or she is highly sensitive to supernatural forces. This term is synonymous with being prophetic or clairvoyant.

Reiki is yet another aspect of being potentially psychic, although it is not restricted to such. Self-healing is an enormous facet of Reiki, although the healing of another can potentially arise from this practice. During Reiki, we utilize universal life force energy (some term this as "God" or "the Absolute") in order to heal the chakras and to gain insight into what needs to be energetically cleared from our spiritual bodies.

Divination can make use of psychic abilities also. It is a method of providing insight into given situations and enabling us to potentially foretell the future based upon current life habits or patterns. Divination techniques vary, but the most common ones include the Tarot, astrology, or the Ouija board.

Astrology can provide a great deal of wisdom when it comes to psychic development. Known as a form of divination that is based upon studying the movement of the celestial bodies, there are many energies and placements of each of the planets that play a major role in unearthing our true ability to understand the psychic world. The twelve signs of the zodiac based upon our birth charts also play a role in this.

Automatic writing enables us to formulate brand new understandings about the psychic world as well as the world around us in ways that may not be obvious to our conscious minds. Given that we are channeling spirits, we may not have an active comprehension of the knowledge that we are gaining about the psychic world, but nevertheless it is there.

Crystals, much like Reiki energy, help us to get in touch with the healing energies that are embedded within them. If we focus on them for long enough, then they will have distinct properties based upon the individual colors and characteristics that each of them possess. This will enhance our psychic abilities as well.

Tarot card reading, a more specific form of divination, permits us to get in touch with our higher selves as well as to discover further information and insight either about our inner selves or the outer circumstances that surround us. While each Tarot deck is unique, all have the common denominator of the Major Arcana and the Minor Arcana suits. While they are commonly associated with the occult world nowadays, they can also be linked with the development of psychic abilities.

Thank you for reading this book. If it has been a benefit to you in any way, or if you have gained any sort of knowledge in reading through this, please take the time to leave an Amazon review. Know and realize that although not everyone may believe in the world of psychic development, it undeniably exists. I commend you for learning more about the different psychic abilities, and wish you the best of luck on your spiritual journey!

www.ingramcontent.com/pod-product-compliance
Lightning Source LLC
LaVergne TN
LVHW021739060526
838200LV00052B/3359